78 Habits for Daily Brilliance

78 Habits for Daily Brilliance

J.P. Adhikari

JPAdhikari Books™

ISBN: 978-81-992645-2-6

Published by JPAdhikari Books™

This book is intended only for educational and personal development purposes and should not be considered a substitute for professional advice.

First Edition: 2025

Cover design and interior formatting: JPAdhikari Books™

Contents

Introduction

Life can get heavy sometimes. Amid the responsibilities of education, career, personal relationships, and the ongoing effort to figure out what actually matters, it may seem as though you are constantly striving for balance, yet never quite attaining it. The world insists, "Do more! Be more! Go big or go home!"

However, genuine transformation may not

be found in extraordinary actions, but in the consistent steps that gradually reshape everything.

This book is about those small steps you can apply in your daily life without needing extra time, money, or motivation. They might seem tiny on the surface, but their ripple effect can be huge. Think of them as gentle switches that slowly light up different corners of your life—your mindset, environment, and confidence.

You do not need to overhaul your entire existence or reinvent yourself overnight. You simply need to take one small, intentional step—and then another.

These habits are written for all those who senses there is more to life, but may be uncertain where to begin. Whether your aim is to build healthier routines, cultivate self-assurance, pursue your goals with clarity, or rediscover joy in the everyday, this book serves as a gentle guide along that journey.

Each section focuses on a single theme. In each section, you will find practical ideas to experiment with, reflections to contemplate, and sparks of insight to keep the journey light, because personal growth need not always feel so serious.

How to Use This Book:

- ***Start Small***
  Begin with a single habit. Allow it to settle into your routine before introducing another.

- ***Be Curious, Not Critical***
  If a day is missed, don't be concerned. Progress is built on patience and self-understanding, not perfection.

- ***Track Your Wins***
  Use the habit tracker to observe your small victories. Even the smallest progress deserves recognition.

- ***Make It Yours***
  Every person's rhythm is different. Adapt the habits to fit your lifestyle and values so they feel natural to you.

Remember, there is no single right pace for growth. You are learning, adjusting, and evolving in your own time, and that is enough.

Intentional Beginnings

Before you chase goals, build routines, or try to "fix" your life—start with your mind. Because your mindset shapes the way you see everything.

This section focuses on small, intentional shifts that create meaningful change. There is no pressure to be perfect; only gentle practices intended to cultivate clarity, calm, and balance in daily life.

Most of these habits take no more than a few minutes. However, those moments can shift the way you think, feel, and move through the world. And over time, these gentle shifts can reshape your life in ways that last.

Habit 1: Start Your Day with a "Why"

Before reaching for your phone or beginning your morning routine, pause for a moment and ask yourself:

"Why am I getting up today?"

Perhaps it is to learn something new, to be present for someone you care about, or to take a small step toward a long-term goal. Starting the day with a clear purpose, even a modest one, lends intention to everything that follows. Without a "why", the day can feel like motion without meaning; with it, you move with purpose.

Habit 2: Ask Yourself, "What's the Best That Could Happen?"

Many of us begin the day anticipating what might go wrong. Consider shifting this perspective. Instead, ask yourself:

> *"What is the best that could happen today?"*

This simple habit broadens your outlook and subtly redirects attention from worry to possibility.

Habit 3: Use the "What Would Future Me Do?" Trick

When you feel stuck, unmotivated, or tempted to give up, pause for a moment and ask yourself:

> *"What would future me want me to do right now?"*

This habit trains your brain to think long-term—like a wiser, more grown version of yourself. It is not about striving for perfection, but about making choices you will later take pride in.

Habit 4: Limit Complaining to Thirty Seconds

Life inevitably presents challenges, and it is natural to feel frustrated or to express those feelings. The key is to set a boundary. Allow yourself thirty seconds to acknowledge and release the frustration—then move forward. Say what you need to say, feel it fully, and then redirect your energy.

For example:

- "This situation is difficult, and I'm frustrated."

- Pause.
- “Alright... what can I do about it?”

In this way, you are not suppressing your emotions; you are acknowledging them without allowing them to dominate your mindset. That is genuine emotional strength in practice.

Habit 5: Take a Two-Minute Gratitude Pause

Take two minutes to be still. Close your eyes or look out the window, and think of three things you are grateful for.

For example:

- The warmth of your morning tea.
- A kind message from a friend.
- The simple fact that you are alive and breathing.

Gratitude is not about pretending that everything is perfect; it is about acknowledging what is already good.

This simple change in mindset moves the mind from focusing on what is missing to appreciating what is present.

Habit 6: Do Something Slightly Uncomfortable

Take a small step beyond your comfort zone—perhaps by taking a cold shower, speaking up in a discussion, or initiating a conversation with someone new.

Challenging your comfort zone, even in modest ways, strengthens mental resilience. It sends a clear message to your mind:

> *"I do not avoid challenges; I rise to meet them."*

Over time, this simple habit transforms apprehension into motivation and help you grow in ways you might not have anticipated.

Habit 7: Give Yourself a Daily Pep Talk

You are your own greatest source of encouragement. So, use that power intentionally. Each morning, take a moment to meet your eyes in the mirror and speak words that are bold, kind, or steady, such as:

- "I am capable of remarkable things."
- "Today, I move with confidence and purpose."
- "Whatever comes my way, I will rise above it."

It may feel unfamiliar at first, but your mind responds to the words you consistently repeat. A daily pep talk is more than a simple ritual—it is a quiet practice of self-trust. Speak gently, speak sincerely, and over time, you will begin to believe what you say.

Habit 8: Smile at Yourself

Even in the mornings, when you feel tired, or not at your best, take a moment to look in the mirror and smile. This small gesture sends a message of calm and care to the mind. It eases tension, elevates mood, and nurtures self-acceptance. Over time, this simple act becomes a gentle reminder that you are still here, still showing up, and still worthy of kindness.

Habit 9: Expand Your Vocabulary

Words shape the way you think. The more you know, the more clearly you can express yourself—and the more confident you feel.

Making a habit of learning a new word each day quietly sharpens your mind and strengthens your voice.

Habit 10: Move Freely for Two Minutes

Before the day's responsibilities draw you in, pause for a moment to reconnect with yourself.

Play your favorite music and allow your body to move naturally, in whatever way feels right. Even two minutes of movement can relieve tension, elevate mood, and increase energy.

Give it a try—you may find yourself smiling before the song ends.

Habit 11: Make Your Bed with Confidence

Making your bed is more than just about tidiness—it creates a sense of order and self-respect at the very start of your day. This simple act becomes your first accomplishment of the day, reminding you that progress begins with the smallest choices.

It also sends a clear message to your mind:

- "I respect my space."
- "I finish what I start."
- "I can create order, even when life feels chaotic."

Habit 12: Keep a "Done" List

To-do lists often highlight what remains unfinished. In contrast, a "done" list draws attention to what you have already accomplished.

At the end of each day, record three achievements, no matter how big or small.

This simple habit builds momentum instead of pressure. It gently shifts your focus from “I didn’t do enough” to “I made progress”. That’s how confidence grows—one small win at a time.

Habit 13: Set One Goal for the Day

Commit to accomplishing one goal today.

Ask yourself:

> *“What is the one task that would make today feel successful?”*

Concentrating on a single goal brings clarity, purpose, and a sense of calm to your day.

Final Thoughts

Your mindset functions as your internal operating system. Even subtle shifts in thought patterns can influence the way you experience the world. These thirteen habits support you in:

- Reframing negative thoughts
- Cultivating self-belief
- Strengthening focus
- Enhancing emotional resilience

Consider them as small, daily rituals of personal empowerment. When practiced consistently, they gradually operate in the background, allowing you to engage with life intentionally rather than respond impulsively.

Smart Living

Smart living is not about being perfect or staying productive all the time. It is about creating a life that works for you—with less stress, more clarity, and choices that truly matter.

In this section, you will explore a series of small, practical habits that help you:

- Stay organized without feeling overwhelmed

- Save time and energy for what truly matters
- Cut through mental clutter and find focus
- Establish routines that harmonize with your lifestyle

Think of these as gentle upgrades to daily living—simple and grounding practices that make life feel a little lighter and a little smarter.

Habit 14: Apply the "Two-Minute Rule"

If a task takes less than two minutes, do it immediately. It may be the email that you have been avoiding, the cup that needs rinsing, or the idea waiting to be written down.

Tiny tasks may seem small, but when you delay them, they accumulate and create mental clutter.

The two-minute rule helps clear that clutter, regain focus, and build momentum.

Habit 15: Clear Your Physical Space for a few Minutes

Your environment influences how you feel. Clutter doesn't just take up space—it drains focus and energy, even when you don't realize it.

Take a few minutes to bring a little order to your surroundings:

- Get rid of the stuff you don't need.
- Put things back where they belong.
- Wipe down your desk or table.

It doesn't have to look perfect. You're simply creating a space that supports you instead of distracting you.

Habit 16: Set a Timer for Screen Breaks

Screens are an integral part of daily life, yet both the mind and the body require regular pauses to rest and recover. Excess screen time can deplete focus, strain the eyes, and leave you feeling fatigued and tense.

Begin with small, intentional breaks.

For example:

- Every 30 minutes, look away for 30 seconds.
- Every hour or so, take a 5-minute off-screen break.
- Use a timer, an app, or a visible reminder to prompt these pauses.

Stretch. Breathe. Blink. Move. Sip some water.

Just a few mindful minutes can restore your energy and help you return to your tasks feeling clearer, calmer, and more focused.

Habit 17: Pick One Task at a Time

Multitasking may feel productive; however, it often fragments attention and disperses energy. Meaningful progress comes from dedicating your full attention to a single purposeful task at a time.

Each morning, choose a single task that actually matters. It might be:

- Writing a report
- Practicing a new skill
- Studying with full focus for an hour

Silence distractions. Set your phone aside. Allow yourself to engage fully.

This habit is not about doing more—it is about doing what matters most with clarity, presence, and intention.

Habit 18: Plan Tomorrow Tonight

Before going to bed, take just five minutes to look ahead.

Ask yourself:

> *"What is the one task I want to accomplish tomorrow? What may feel challenging, and how can I make it easier?"*

Write it down. Prepare your clothes for the next day. Charge your devices.

These small, intentional actions help your mind unwind and allow tomorrow to begin with greater ease and clarity.

Habit 19: Create a Morning Cue

Mornings need not be dramatic—they only require a small signal indicating:

> *"It's time to start the day."*

A morning cue is a small, repeatable action that initiates your daily routine.

For example:

- Open the curtains and let in the light
- Brew your preferred tea or coffee
- Play a playlist that puts you in a good mood
- Step outside for a few deep breaths of fresh air

You don't need a long ritual; just one simple trigger is enough. With time, this simple act becomes a mental switch that gently moves you from sleepy to ready, calm, and focused.

Habit 20: Organize One Thing Weekly

A complete life overhaul is unnecessary; small, incremental steps are sufficient.

Each week, select a single item or area to organize.

For example:

- Clean out one drawer
- Sort your desktop folders
- Organize your bookshelf
- Declutter your phone applications
- Organize your digital notes

These modest and consistent efforts build confidence and gradually create a more orderly and manageable life.

Habit 21: Batch the Boring Stuff

Certain tasks may feel tedious.

Rather than scattering them throughout your day and depleting your energy, consider batching them together.

Pick one block of time to tackle things like:

- Paying bills
- Responding to emails
- Running errands
- Preparing meals for the week

By minimizing mental switching, stress is naturally reduced. This approach conserves energy and allows you to focus on the tasks that matter most.

Habit 22: Give Your Day a Theme

When each day feels like a blur of disconnected tasks, maintaining focus on what truly matters becomes challenging.

Consider assigning a theme to each day.

When your attention has a clear direction, decision fatigue diminishes, and your days begin to feel more structured and intentional.

For example:

- Monday: Planning and Priorities
- Tuesday: Learning and Skill-Building
- Wednesday: Deep Work
- Thursday: Health and Self-Care
- Friday: Social and Follow-Ups
- Saturday: Errands and Home
- Sunday: Rest and Reset

A simple daily theme can transform ordinary days into ones that are calmer, more focused, and purposeful.

Habit 23: Use the "No List"

Life is not just shaped by what you say "yes" to; it's equally defined by what you choose to say "no" to.

A "No List" is a short, personal reminder of things you're intentionally avoiding to protect your time, energy, and peace of mind.

Your ”No List” may include:

- No phones during meals
- No checking emails before 10 AM
- No toxic gossip
- No saying “yes” when you mean “maybe”
- No scrolling in bed

This practice is not about restriction—it is about clarity, focus, and self-respect. Each intentional “no” creates additional space for what truly matters to you.

Sometimes, saying “no” is the most effective way to affirm yourself and prioritize your well-being.

Habit 24: Brain Dump Before Bed

If your mind spins at night, this habit will help.

Before going to bed, take a notebook or use an app to record everything on your mind—no particular structure is required.

Include:

- Tasks left unfinished
- Ideas you wish to remember
- Worries, reminders, or random thoughts

This practice clears your mental space, allowing your brain to rest more effectively.

No more clutter keeping you awake—just a calm mind, ready to recharge.

Habit 25: Keep a Digital "Idea Jar"

Great ideas rarely arrive on schedule.

They often strike in random moments—during a walk, in the shower, or while waiting in line.

Do not let them slip away—capture them immediately.

Create a digital "idea jar" using:

- Your notes app
- A quick voice memo
- An email to yourself

Record everything that comes to your mind:

- Business ideas
- Gift ideas
- Book titles
- Long-term aspirations

Review your collection weekly and continue to add to it.

This practice is not about judging your ideas; it is about preserving and nurturing them.

A seemingly disorganized idea jar today could become the source of your next significant breakthrough tomorrow.

Habit 26: Start a "Little Wins" Jar

Big goals take time, but the small victories along the way keep you moving forward. Take a moment to acknowledge and celebrate those victories and notice how much progress you are making.

Grab a jar, a box, or even a digital note, and start recording your little wins—the moments you are proud of, no matter how small.

For example, you might record the following:

- "I made my bed every day this week."
- "I said no to something that didn't feel right."
- "I finally sent that email I had been avoiding."

Add each achievement to your collection as it occurs. Over time, these entries will form a meaningful chronicle of your persistence and personal evolution.

Why this habit matters:

- It shifts your focus toward what is working.
- It boosts motivation by showing your progress along the way.
- On tough days, you'll have a collection of reminders that you are doing better than you realize.

Final Thoughts

Smart living is about making small, intentional choices that make your days lighter, faster, and less stressful.

You have now explored thirteen microhabits designed to help you:

- Simplify your daily routines
- Conserve and channel mental energy effectively

- Spend time where it truly matters
- Stay productive—without burning out

Each of these habits requires only a few moments to practice. As you stack them together, you start building a life that feels more in control, calm, and focused.

The Self-Care Blueprint

A true self-care journey is not only about relaxation or appearance—it is about leveling up in ways that make you feel unstoppable. The kind of glow that radiates from the inside out.

In this section, you will explore simple yet powerful habits designed to:

- Strengthen your confidence and self-image
- Enhance both physical and mental well-being
- Support meaningful goal-setting and consistent follow-through
- Sustain motivation and momentum, even during low-energy phases

Each of these practices represents an uplifting change that helps you appear as your most balanced and empowered self.

Let's begin.

Habit 27: Hydrate Yourself Right After Waking Up

After waking up—and before having tea or coffee—hydrate yourself.

Your body wakes up slightly dehydrated after 7–8 hours of sleep. A simple glass of water ignites your brain function, boosts your energy, enhances your skin's glow, and supports digestion.

You can even add a slice of lemon for a refreshing flavor.

This tiny habit signals to your body:

> *"I am taking care of myself today."*

Habit 28: Stretch for At least Two Minutes in the Morning

A quick morning stretch helps:

- Wake up stiff muscles
- Improve blood flow and posture
- Release stress from sleep
- Center your mind before the day begins

This habit is not about executing perfect yoga poses. Simply move your body: roll your shoulders, gently twist your spine, and take several deep, mindful breaths.

Self-care depends on the way you begin each day.

Habit 29: Eat at Least One Colorful Food Daily

Try adding colorful foods to your plate every day—your body will love it.

Fruits and vegetables like berries, carrots, spinach, peppers, and mangoes are packed with vitamins, fiber, and natural goodness. Each color offers its own unique benefits.

For example:

- Orange — supports skin and eye health
- Purple — boosts brain power
- Green — strengthens energy and immunity
- Red — promotes heart health

- Yellow — aids digestion and uplifts mood

Even one colorful addition makes a difference.

Habit 30: Breathe Deeply Before You Eat

Before you take your first bite of the day, take a deep, slow breath.

This mindful pause:

- Calms your body and mind
- Helps you notice true hunger and fullness
- Makes each meal more peaceful and satisfying

With time, this single breath turns mealtime into a small moment of gratitude.

Your body and your mood will feel the difference.

Habit 31: Take a Ten-Minute Walk Every Day

You don't need fancy equipment or a gym membership to move your body. Walk for at least ten minutes a day.

This simple habit can help you with:

- A clearer mind
- A better mood
- A more energized body
- A calmer nervous system
- Improved digestion

A 10-minute walk is self-respect in motion.

Habit 32: Try a 5-Day Sugar Break

Sugar isn't the enemy, but too much of it can drain your energy and dull your glow.

Give your body a break with a simple five-day sugar pause.

During this period, you may experience:

- Clearer, healthier-looking skin
- Improved sleep quality
- More consistent energy levels

You don't have to do it forever—think of it as a quick reset for your body. Discipline now brings radiance soon.

Habit 33: Set a Bedtime Alarm

We set alarms to wake up—but why not one to help us wind down?

Sleep is when your body repairs, your brain resets, and your mood stabilizes—but we often scroll, snack, and stall until it's midnight again.

Set an alarm 30–60 minutes before bed that says:

> *"It's time to slow down."*

Pair it with a gentle ritual, such as dimming the lights or writing down a few thoughts.

Better rest means a brighter you.

Habit 34: Wash Your Face Before Bed

Real glow-ups don't come from fancy routines—they come from small acts of consistency. Take a moment to wash your face, even when you're tired.

This simple habit:

- Clears away the dirt, oil, and stress of the day.

- Helps prevent breakouts and dullness.
- Signals your brain that it's time to rest.
- Builds discipline in just a few minutes.

Habit 35: Use a Scent You Love

One of the easiest ways to shift your mood is through scent. Whether it's spraying a favorite perfume, using an essential oil, or a scented lotion—let yourself enjoy a smell that makes you feel good. It could remind you of calm mornings, cozy nights, or happy memories.

Scents like lavender can help you unwind, citrus can refresh your mind, and vanilla can bring a sense of comfort.

Whatever you choose, make it something that feels like a little gift to yourself. Over time, certain scents will become your personal "reset" button, grounding you whenever life gets hectic.

Habit 36: Have One Go-To Outfit That Makes You Feel Amazing

Sometimes, all it takes is one outfit that makes you stand taller and smile wider.

Choose something that:

- Boosts your confidence
- Reflects your personal style
- Works in different situations
- Feels effortless to wear

Keep it clean. Keep it ready.

This isn't about fashion, it's about confidence. When you feel good, you move differently.

Your go-to outfit becomes your go-to energy.

Habit 37: Compliment Someone Daily

Compliments need not be grand; they can be quiet expressions of kindness offered to others, even in your mind. Each day, observe something admirable in someone—be it a friend, family member, classmate, colleague, or even a stranger. Notice their smile, their effort, or the way they carry themselves.

For instance, you may say aloud or silently think:

- "You're doing great"
- "That was kind"
- "I like your style"

Giving compliments lifts others up—and it lifts you, too. It trains your mind to focus on the good around you and spreads positive vibes.

Try it today and see how it changes your mood and the way you see the world.

Habit 38: Create a "Hype File"

We all need reminders of our brilliance.

A "Hype File" is your personal collection of encouragement—digital or physical.

A hype file may include:

- Compliments people have given you
- Achievements or awards you're proud of
- Positive notes or messages from friends and family
- Photos that make you smile
- Motivational quotes or songs that inspire and energize you

Whenever you're feeling down, doubting yourself, or just need some extra confidence, open your hype file and soak in those good vibes.

Building this habit helps you remember your strengths and lifts your mood, especially on difficult days.

Habit 39: Learn One Simple Recipe

Cooking doesn't have to be complicated. Start with one easy recipe you enjoy. It could be a quick stir-fry, a simple salad, or a basic sandwich. Make it a few times until you're confident.

Knowing how to cook even one meal means that you can take care of yourself without relying on others.

It is also a fun skill to show off to family and friends!

Experiment with this habit; you might discover that you actually enjoy it.

Habit 40: Pick a Power Phrase and Repeat It Daily

A power phrase is a short, positive sentence you say to yourself to boost confidence and focus. It could be something like:

- "I've got this."
- "I am enough."
- "Keep moving forward."

Choose a phrase that feels right for you and repeat it every day. Saying your power phrase helps train your mind to stay positive, specifically during tough moments.

With time, it becomes a mental boost that you can rely on whenever you need additional focus and strength.

Identify your power phrase, recite it consistently each day, and observe how it gradually elevates your mood and strengthens your mindset.

Final Thoughts

True self-care is not about perfection, it is about consistent progress.

These small habits help you nurture confidence and care for yourself.

Each represents a step toward achieving your full potential.

Remember, a meaningful transformation occurs gradually.

Approach these practices with patience and gentleness. Over time, you will notice not only outward changes, but also a stronger sense of self-love and an enduring inner radiance.

Continue to nurture yourself. Continue growing. Your inner glow will guide and sustain you.

Interpersonal Intelligence

Getting along with others is one of the most valuable skills you can have.

In this section, we will explore simple, practical habits to strengthen your communication, empathy, and confidence in social situations. Whether you want to navigate difficult conversations, or simply feel more at ease around people, these habits will guide you toward more genuine and fulfilling connections.

Let's get started!

Habit 41: Initiate the Greeting

It may feel a little uncomfortable, but saying "hello" first can totally change the energy in a room. A simple greeting—whether in a classroom, workplace, or just passing by someone—shows confidence, warmth, and openness.

Most people wait for someone else to make the first move. When you take that tiny step, you open the door to smiles, friendly exchanges, and even meaningful new connections. You do not need perfect words. A smile and a simple "Hey!" or "What's up?" is enough.

Make it a daily practice to be the one who breaks silence with kindness. You never know how much a single word can brighten someone's day—including yours.

Habit 42: Use People's Names When You Talk to Them

Using someone's name in conversation is a simple but powerful way to connect. When you say a person's name, it grabs their attention, shows respect, and makes the interaction feel more personal. It helps build trust and makes people feel valued because their name is a big part of their identity. Try to remember names and use them naturally when you greet someone, ask a question, or share a compliment. This small habit can make your conversations friendlier and leave a positive impression.

Habit 43: Maintain Effective Eye Contact

Eye contact is one of the simplest yet most powerful ways to convey attentiveness and genuine interest during a conversation. Aim to hold eye contact for a few seconds at a time—it helps establish trust, confidence, and mutual respect.

Although it may feel slightly uncomfortable at first, with consistent practice it becomes natural and strengthens your interpersonal connections. Maintaining appropriate eye contact not only demonstrates respect but also allows others to feel seen, heard, and valued.

Try it today—you may be surprised by how much it enhances the quality of your interactions.

Habit 44: Remember Meaningful Details About Others

One of the simplest ways to make others feel acknowledged and valued is to remember a small detail about them. It could be their favorite food, a hobby they mentioned, the name of their pet, or something they were looking forward to recently. The next time you meet, refer to it in conversation.

For instance:

- “How was your trip to the mountains?”
- “Did your dog recover?”
- “Still playing guitar these days?”

Recalling small details demonstrates genuine attentiveness and care. It strengthens relationships, build trust, and brings warmth to every interaction.

Habit 45: Mirror Others’ Energy with Respect

One of the simplest ways to connect with others is to gently reflect their energy. If someone is calm and composed, adopt a softer tone. If they are lively and enthusiastic, bring a touch of warmth and engagement to your words.

Mirroring someone's vibe shows that you're in sync with them—it builds comfort, trust, and better communication. However, always do so with sincerity and respect. Keep it authentic. There is no need to force excitement or pretend to be someone you are not.

Meet people at their level, with kindness and presence. Over time, this practice enables you to engage more naturally and helps others feel seen and understood.

Habit 46: Ask Follow-Up Questions

When someone is talking, asking a follow-up question shows that you're really listening and interested. Instead of just saying "Okay" or "Cool," try to ask something that encourages them to share more.

For example, if they say they went to a concert, you can ask:

- "What was your favorite song they played?"
- "Who did you go with?"

Follow-up questions make conversations more meaningful. They help you connect better and show that you care.

Try it out next time you chat.

Habit 47: Practice "The Pause" Before Responding

Before responding in a conversation, particularly during emotional or important moments, take a brief pause of one or two seconds. This short pause allows your mind to process information, think clearly, and respond with intention rather than reacting impulsively.

Practicing this habit can help you avoid saying something you might later regret and ensures that your responses are measured, thoughtful, and composed. Whether you are answering a question, responding to feedback, or engaging in casual conversation, that little moment of silence can make a big difference.

Habit 48: Practice Concise Communication

When engaging in conversation, aim to keep your responses or stories to approximately one or two minutes. This approach helps keep the conversation balanced and interesting, ensuring that both participants have an opportunity to contribute without one person dominating.

Furthermore, it encourages clarity and conciseness, making your message easier to understand and follow. If you notice the other person's attention waning, conclude your point and invite them to contribute.

Habit 49: Know When to Exit a Conversation

Not every conversation needs to last forever—and that's okay. Sometimes, the energy fades. The topic is done. Or the other person seems distracted. That's your cue to end the conversation politely and with confidence.

For example, you might say:

- "It was great talking to you!"
- "It's time for me to go, but let's catch up again soon."

Habit 50: Offer Specific Compliments

Rather than giving a general compliment such as "Nice job" or "You look good," focus on highlighting a particular quality, action, or effort that you genuinely appreciate.

For instance, you might say:

- "I really appreciate how clearly you explained that idea—it made it easy to understand."
- "Your smile lights up the room and creates a welcoming atmosphere."
- "You handled that situation with remarkable calm and confidence."

Specific compliments feel more genuine because they show you're paying attention to the little things that make someone unique. When you give detailed praise, it can boost the other person's confidence.

People remember when you notice and appreciate their real efforts or qualities. Try making it a habit to look for these details in your friends, family, or classmates. Thoughtful compliments not only brighten their day but also create positive vibes around you.

Habit 51: Celebrate Others Out Loud

When someone achieves something noteworthy, whether a friend earns high grades, a sibling completes a project, or a coworker excels at a task, acknowledge it verbally. Expressing your recognition demonstrates that you notice and appreciate their effort.

For example, you might say:

- "You delivered that presentation exceptionally well!"
- "That was an impressive decision—you handled it brilliantly!"

Celebrating others out loud not only uplifts them but also strengthens your relationships. It creates a positive environment where people feel recognized and valued.

Furthermore, genuine appreciation often invites the same kindness in return.

Habit 52: Say "Thank You" Instead of Apologizing So Much

It is easy to fall into the habit of over-apologizing, even when you have not done anything wrong. Instead of saying "Sorry I'm late", try "Thank you for waiting". Instead of "Sorry for talking so much", try "Thank you for listening".

Shifting from apology to gratitude changes the tone of your words. It makes you sound more confident and helps others feel appreciated, not uncomfortable.

Start by noticing how often you say "sorry" out of habit and gradually replace it with genuine expressions of thanks. This small change nurtures self-respect and strengthens the quality of your interactions.

Habit 53: Speak Kindly About Others in Their Absence

It is easy to fall into gossip. Yet, there is greater strength in choosing kindness when someone is not present. Speaking positively about others, even when they are not around to hear it, reflects integrity and generosity of spirit.

You may:

- Compliment a friend to someone else.
- Defend someone's effort or character.
- Mention how someone inspires you even if they'll never hear it.

Consistently practicing this habit not only empowers others, but also cultivates a refined mindset grounded in respect, trust, and authenticity.

Habit 54: Don't Interrupt—Even When You're Excited

When a conversation gets interesting, it is easy to jump in, especially if you relate or have a story of your own. However, interrupting, even out of excitement, can make the other person feel like their words do not matter.

Instead, try the following:

- Pause. Let them finish their sentence or story.
- Listen fully. Focus on understanding them, not just waiting for your turn.
- Record the idea, either mentally or in writing, and retain it if it is important.

When you give someone the space to finish, you show respect, emotional intelligence, and patience. You become the kind of person people feel safe talking to.

Habit 55: Ask for Help Without Apologizing

You do not need to apologize for seeking help. Asking for support is a sign of strength, not weakness. It reflects self-awareness, humility, and a willingness to learn and grow.

Instead of saying:

- "Sorry to bother you, but..."

Try saying:

- "Could you help me with this?"
- "I would greatly appreciate your guidance."

Leading with an apology may unintentionally suggest that your needs are burdensome. Maintain politeness while asserting confidence when requesting support.

Habit 56: Respect the Group Chat Vibe

Every group chat has its own rhythm—some are for jokes and casual banter, while others focus on updates and important plans.

Before sending a long message or a random meme, take a moment to evaluate the conversation.

Ask yourself:

> *"Is this the right place and time for this?"*

Respecting the chat's vibe demonstrates emotional intelligence and helps you become the kind of participant others genuinely enjoy interacting with.

Habit 57: Learn to Laugh at Yourself

Spilled coffee on your shirt?

Sent a message to the wrong chat?

Forgotten what you were saying mid-sentence?

These things are perfectly normal; such occurrences happen to most of us. Rather than feeling embarrassed or defensive, try to laugh them off.

When you can smile at your own minor mistakes, you reduce their impact. Laughing at yourself does not indicate a lack of seriousness—it demonstrates that you are comfortable with your own humanity.

Habit 58: Set One Small Boundary and Honor It

Boundaries need not be dramatic; they can be simple, subtle, and life-enhancing.

Choose one boundary that protects your peace, focus, or well-being, and commit to maintaining it. Hold it gently but firmly. You do not need to justify it to anyone or seek permission. You simply need to respect what you truly need.

Final Thoughts

Being good with people is not about being the loudest in the room or always having the perfect words. It is about listening, showing respect, and being genuinely present. These small habits build trust, connection, and warmth. They help others feel seen, safe, and valued in your presence.

When you practice interpersonal skills with kindness and intention, your relationships grow richer, calmer, and more authentic. Whether you are communicating with a friend or meeting someone new, you hold the power to improve the moment. Continue showing up with sincerity; it makes more of a difference than you may realize.

Flow of Creation

Creativity is something everyone carries within. It shapes how you solve problems, generate new ideas, decorate your surroundings, style your outfits, or even craft the perfect message to a friend.

This section is about unlocking that creative energy within you — without pressure to be perfect. It is about curiosity and making space for your uniqueness to shine.

You don't need expensive tools, fancy materials, or hours of free time. All it takes is a few minutes a day to explore, experiment, or observe the world around you in a fresh way.

When you connect with your creative energy, you:

- Elevate your mood and reduce stress
- Learn new ways to express yourself
- Find inspiration in everyday moments
- Gain confidence by trusting your own ideas

Whether you choose to draw, write, dance, cook, or think in new ways, this section will help you explore the potential of your creative flow.

Habit 59: Create Something Small Every Day

You don't have to make a masterpiece every time. The true value lies in showing up and creating something meaningful, no matter how small.

Whether it's a few lines in a journal, a short poem, a simple meal, or even a playlist of songs you love. These little acts of creation keep your imagination alive.

Engaging in creative acts each day helps you to:

- Train your mind to think in new and flexible ways
- Elevate your mood and reduce stress
- Build confidence by valuing progress over perfection
- Open pathways to larger ideas and projects

Remember, creativity is not measured by how impressive something appears, but by the joy and curiosity it evokes in you.

With time, these small daily creations accumulate, shaping a life that feels vibrant and expressive.

Habit 60: Doodle During Boring Moments

Boring moments can feel like wasted time, but they do not have to be.

Keep a small notebook or scrap of paper handy and use those moments to doodle, such as sketching shapes, drawing little characters, or writing down random ideas.

Why doodling matters:

- It keeps your mind active and engaged
- It sparks creativity in unexpected ways
- It helps reduce stress and boredom

- It can improve focus and memory during long talks or lectures
- It's a simple and enjoyable way to express yourself

Don't worry about how it looks. There is no right or wrong way to doodle. Let your hand move freely and see what emerges.

Over time, your doodles might turn into bigger ideas or inspiring new projects.

Habit 61: Carry a Tiny Notebook

Big ideas don't always show up at convenient times. That's why having a small notebook can be a game-changer.

Keep it simple, something that fits in your pocket or bag.

Use it to:

- Note down random thoughts or quotes
- Scribble ideas for stories, songs, or projects

- Capture dreams, moods, or questions
- Track tiny moments that made you smile

Why this habit matters:

- It trains you to notice and value your own thoughts
- It gives your creativity a place to land
- It helps you stay present and reflective throughout the day
- It becomes a personal archive of inspiration over time

There is no need to make it perfect; simply make it your own — a space that awaits whenever inspiration stirs or emotion arises.

Your mind holds countless treasures; all you need is a safe place to gather and keep them.

Habit 62: Keep a "Weird Ideas" Note in Your Phone

Some of the most remarkable creative breakthroughs begin as thoughts that seem unusual. When an unexpected idea or question arises, it is a small treasure worth preserving.

Create a dedicated note or folder on your phone solely for these "weird ideas". The next time an unconventional notion appears, record it immediately. Avoid overthinking; simply capture the spark as it appears.

Why this habit matters:

- It trains your mind to notice and value original thinking
- It prevents good ideas from fading unnoticed
- It builds a personal archive of inspiration to revisit anytime

- Many great projects begin as small, unconventional thoughts

Do not worry if your ideas feel incomplete or eccentric. Creativity often begins in untidy form, and that is perfectly natural.

Over time, you may begin to notice connections, recurring themes, and new directions emerging from your growing collection.

In addition, giving your thoughts a place to land frees your mind to rest and refocus.

Keep your "weird ideas" note close at hand. Your next significant breakthrough may be only a few lines away.

Habit 63: End a Creative Session by Saving One Idea for Later

When you conclude a creative session—whether writing, sketching, brainstorming, or engaging in another form of expression—

make it a practice to preserve at least one idea to revisit later.

It may be a thought that did not fit today, a new perspective to explore, or a spark that requires time to mature.

Why this habit matters:

- It allows your creativity to continue flowing beyond the session
- It gives your mind something to anticipate in the next session
- It helps prevent creative fatigue by pacing your ideas
- It gradually builds a personal reservoir of inspiration

Before stepping away, record that one idea and set it aside. When you return, you will find fresh momentum waiting—and that sense of continuity can make all the difference.

Habit 64: Craft a Board for Your Aspirations

Every dream begins as a vision before it takes shape in reality. Crafting a board for your aspirations serves as a bridge between imagination and manifestation,transforming abstract ideas into something you can see and feel.

Whether your aspiration involves creating a project, building a business, redesigning a space, or reimagining yourself, gather images, colors, words, and textures that capture the essence of your vision.

You may:

- Use a digital tool or a physical board.
- Combine screenshots, sketches, or quotes that inspire you.
- Include fabrics, color swatches, or any elements that evoke emotion or clarity.

Why this habit matters:

- It transforms abstract aspirations into tangible form.
- It sustains focus, motivation, and emotional engagement.
- It serves as a visual affirmation that your dream is worthy of pursuit.
- It inspires fresh ideas, styles, and creative directions.

This practice is not about perfection; it is about resonance. Allow your imagination to lead, and craft a board that quietly declares:

"This is what I want to create. This is what it could become."

Then, let that vision draw you steadily closer to achieving your goal.

Habit 65: Explore Beyond Your Familiar Sphere

It is easy to settle into routines where you read, watch, or listen to the same types of content day after day. Although familiarity feels safe, it can limit your growth and creativity.

Challenge yourself to explore something entirely different from your usual interests. For example, read a book from an unfamiliar genre, listen to a podcast on a topic you know little about, experience music from another culture, or watch a movie offering perspectives different from your own.

Why this habit matters:

- It broadens your worldview and strengthen your understanding of people with diverse backgrounds and beliefs

- It ignites new ideas and creative insights by exposing you to unfamiliar voices and storytelling styles

- It challenges assumptions and opens your mind to alternative possibilities

- It may lead to the discovery of new passions, hobbies, or perspectives that enrich your life

- It cultivates empathy by connecting you with experiences you might never encounter otherwise

At first, this exploration may feel unusual or even uncomfortable, but that is where growth begins.

Commit to maintaining this practice with regularity, even in modest forms. Gradually, your curiosity will broaden, your creativity will attain greater depth, and your understanding of the world will evolve with increasing sophistication.

Habit 66: Observe the Process of Creation

Have you ever wondered how things come into being? Whether it is a loaf of bread, a music composition, or a handcrafted chair, witnessing the process of creation can be both captivating and inspiring.

Take time to observe how something is made—from beginning to completion.

For example, you can observe:

- A behind-the-scenes video of a film or performance
- A time-lapse of an artist at work
- A detailed cooking demonstration
- A craftsperson shaping an object by hand
- A designer transforming an idea into form

Why this habit matters:

- It reveals that every finished work begins in imperfection

- It cultivates appreciation for detail, patience, and craftsmanship

- It can ignite curiosity and inspire new creative pursuits

- It shifts your perception from "I could never do that" to "Perhaps I could try".

There is a quiet beauty in the act of making. Observing others create not only enhances your appreciation for the process, but may also awaken the impulse to create within yourself.

Stay curious, observe with attention, and allow the process to inspire your own creations.

Habit 67: Revisit Something That Moved You as a Child

There is something powerful about going back to a story, show, or song that once stirred your heart—when you were younger, more open, and full of wonder.

Perhaps it was:

- A book that inspired you to dream big
- A cartoon that made you laugh without restraint
- A movie that brought you to tears, even before you could comprehend its depth
- A song that felt like it got you before anyone else did

Revisiting these experiences now can reconnect you with emotions you may have long forgotten. Such a return is not mere nostalgia; it is an act of remembering the person you once were and acknowledging the distance you have traveled since.

Why this habit matters:

- It reconnects you with your emotional depth and inner child
- It reignites inspiration and a sense of wonder
- It brings comfort and familiarity in a noisy, fast-moving world
- It reminds you of your authentic self before external expectations shaped who you should become

Approach these experiences with renewed awareness. Allow them to move you in ways they once could not. Within their enduring resonance, you may rediscover traces of your most authentic self.

Habit 68: Give Voice to Your Ideas

Your ideas matter, yet they often remain confined to your mind. Expressing them aloud gives them shape, energy, and direction.

Even if no one is around, articulate your thoughts to yourself. Discuss a concept, explain a dream, or brainstorm verbally. You may be surprised by how differently your ideas resonate once they are given voice.

Try the following approaches:

- Record a voice note while thinking through a concept
- Share a preliminary idea with a trusted friend or mentor
- Rehearse your concept aloud as though presenting it

Why this habit matters:

- It builds confidence in your own voice

- It helps clarify jumbled or incomplete thoughts
- It transforms vague notions into actionable possibilities
- It trains you to express ideas clearly and passionately

You don't need a flawless plan, but a willingness to give your ideas a voice. The moment you speak them, they transition from private thoughts to potential realities.

Habit 69: Create Without the Need to Share

In a culture where constant sharing has become the norm, it is easy to become preoccupied with external validation, such as likes, comments, and approval. However, some of the most creative experiences unfold, when no one else is watching.

Try creating something solely for yourself, without the obligation to post it online or present it to others.

Creating in private allows you to:

- Explore ideas freely, without fear of judgment
- Take creative risks that you might avoid in public
- Rediscover the intrinsic joy of creating for its own sake
- Connect with your inner voice and authentic style
- Build confidence by focusing on the process instead of the outcome

This practice reminds you that your creativity possesses worth independent of external recognition. It cultivates a sincere relationship with your craft that is based on self-expression, not validation.

The next time you create something, resist the urge to immediately share it. Keep it private for a while and enjoy that feeling of freedom and discovery.

In time, you may find that this private creativity enriches your growth and leads to more authentic expression when you choose to share.

Habit 70: Give Yourself Permission to Be Bad at It

Not everything you create needs to be impressive. In fact, genuine growth often begins in moments of uncertainty and imperfection.

Engage in activities purely out of curiosity. For example:

- Sketch, even if your lines are uneven
- Dance, even if you lose the rhythm

- Speak, even if your voice trembles

When you release the expectation of mastery, you rediscover the simple joy of creation itself. Within that space lie learning, playfulness, and authentic self-expression.

Why it matters:

- It quiets the fear of failure
- It creates space for exploration rather than performance
- It strengthens self-trust and emotional resilience
- It reminds you that progress often begins with imperfection

You need not excel at something to find meaning in it. Allow yourself to create freely—to make something unconventional, playful, or beautifully flawed. Because what begins as imperfect often becomes the seed of brilliance.

Habit 71: Collaborate with Someone You Admire

Collaboration in harmony often leads to outcomes enriched by mutual respect, shared enthusiasm, and creative synergy.

Seek out an individual whose perspective and values resonate with yours. It may be a friend, a colleague, or even someone you have long admired from a distance.

Engage in a joint project, exchange ideas, or explore possibilities together. Collaboration introduces fresh perspectives, stimulates creativity, and transforms the process into an enriching and enjoyable experience.

Why this habit matters:

- It encourages learning and personal growth through shared insight
- It sustains motivation by turning individual effort into a collective journey

- It creates opportunities for new ideas and skills

Working with someone you admire can transform challenges into shared discoveries and ideas into achievements.

Habit 72: Prioritize Completion Over Perfection

Starting something new is exciting, but true growth emerges in its completion. It is easy to get stuck chasing perfection or abandoning projects when they don't turn out as expected.

Develop the habit of bringing projects to completion, regardless of the outcome. Finishing provides valuable experience and a sense of accomplishment, even if the result seems imperfect or is not fully realized.

Why this habit matters:

- It builds discipline and follow-through

- Greater learning occurs through completion than through endless revision

- It enables you to identify what succeeded and what could be improved for future efforts

- It reduces the fear of failure by showing that imperfection is acceptable

- Each completed project is a stepping stone toward better skills and confidence

Completion is more important than perfection. Perfectionism can keep you stuck forever, whereas completion, however flawed, moves you forward.

Therefore, choose a project and see it through to completion. Celebrate the accomplishment, however modest or imperfect the outcome may be.

Final Thoughts

Creativity is not just something you are born with. It is a capacity that can be cultivated through consistent practice and deliberate effort. Every small habit and act of imagination accumulates over time, illuminating pathways to new ideas and possibilities.

From moments of doodling to thoughtful collaboration, these habits demonstrate that creativity lies in everyday choices. It is about granting yourself permission to explore freely and to find joy in the process itself, rather than in the perfection of the outcome.

Key reminders:

- Creativity often arises unexpectedly; allow space for reflection, daydreaming, and moments of quiet.
- Sharing ideas and collaborating with others can ignite inspiration beyond your expectations.

- Preserving and revisiting your ideas sustains the flow and evolution of creative energy.

Above all, creativity is inherently personal. What ignites your imagination may differ from what inspires another, and that is precisely its beauty.

So, keep experimenting and keep trusting your unique creative voice. Your spark is waiting to grow into something remarkable.

Financial Clarity

Money may not be the ultimate goal, but the way we manage it shapes our sense of freedom, confidence, and long-term security. Whether you are saving for a meaningful objective, seeking to reduce financial stress, or striving for greater control over your resources, cultivating sound financial habits can transform your life.

This section presents the essentials of money

management in clear, actionable steps that anyone can follow. With a willingness to learn and a commitment to consistent, intentional actions, you can build momentum over time and develop a balanced, empowered money mindset.

After all, your relationship with money is as important as the balance you seek to maintain.

Habit 73: Review Your Bank Balance Calmly

Monitoring your bank balance need not be a source of stress or anxiety. Rather than avoiding it or reacting with worry, cultivate a calm and consistent approach.

Establish a routine—daily, or several times a week—to check your balance. View this practice as an opportunity to gain clarity about your financial situation, not as a moment for self-judgment or apprehension.

Why this habit matters:

- It keeps you informed, enabling more deliberate and thoughtful financial decisions.
- It allows you to detect errors or unexpected charges.
- It reduces anxiety by creating a sense of control rather than surprise.
- It gradually builds financial confidence through regular awareness.

As you become more comfortable with this habit, managing your finances becomes simpler and more empowering.

Habit 74: Track One Week of Spending

One of the easiest ways to start gaining control over your finances is by tracking your spending.

For seven consecutive days, record every expense, no matter how small. Include even minor purchases. These often reveal more than you expect.

You may use:

- A simple notebook
- A notes app on your phone

Why this habit matters:

- It provides an accurate view of your spending habits.
- You spot patterns and small expenses you didn't notice before.
- It builds awareness that naturally leads to better financial decisions.
- It allows observation without immediate pressure to change.

The goal here is not to feel guilty, but to understand. Once you become aware of your spending style, you can make thoughtful adjustments that truly last.

Habit 75: Disengage from Sources That Encourage Overspending

Certain sources are highly skilled at capturing attention and inspiring spontaneous purchases. Over time, such exposure can subtly influence your spending and lead to unnecessary purchases.

This habit encourages disengagement from the sources that consistently prompt impulsive spending. Begin with the source that exerts the strongest influence on your purchasing decisions.

Why this habit matters:

- It restores autonomy over personal purchasing choices and motivations.
- It allows continued support for preferred brands, but on self-determined terms.

This practice is not about permanent disengagement, but about establishing deliberate distance. By doing so, you create the mental and emotional space necessary to make thoughtful, intentional financial choices rather than reactive ones.

This habit safeguards both your financial stability and your peace of mind.

Habit 76: Assign a Purpose to Your Money

Financial resources are most effective when allocated with intention. Rather than allowing money to remain idle in your account or to be spent without a structured plan, it is advisable to assign a specific purpose to your money.

This entails determining precisely how each unit of currency should be utilized prior to expenditure or saving.

Why this habit matters:

- It gives you control over your money instead of letting it control you.

- Helps you avoid overspending and makes budgeting much easier.

- Makes sure you're covering all your essentials and priorities first.

- Encourages consistent saving and prevents money from disappearing unnoticed.

- It reduces financial stress by providing a clear overview of monetary allocation.

Start by listing your regular expenses and goals, then allocate your income accordingly. Even a preliminary plan, such as distributing your earnings between designated allocations, can yield significant benefits.

Over time, this habit builds a strong base for healthy money management and financial confidence.

Habit 77: Pause Before Major Purchases

The immediate impulse to acquire something desirable can be compelling; however, acting on such urges too quickly may result in regret or financial indiscretion.

Whenever you are thinking about making a big purchase, or even a small but impulsive one, pause for a few hours before deciding to buy. Allow yourself time to gain perspective.

Why this habit matters:

- It provides mental clarity to determine whether the purchase represents a genuine need or a fleeting desire.
- It helps you avoid emotional spending driven by stress, excitement, or social influence.
- It strengthens financial discipline and improves long-term self-control.

You can simplify the practice of this habit by adopting the following strategies:

- Create a list where you write down items that you want but are not ready to buy.
- Set reminders to revisit the list later to see if you still feel the same.
- Share your plan with a close friend or family member to help keep you accountable.
- Keep in mind that items of genuine importance will not disappear overnight.

This habit turns impulsive spending into thoughtful decision-making and that can save you money and stress in the long run.

Habit 78: Believe That Future You Deserves Wealth

The way you think about money today shapes your financial reality in the future.

When you truly believe that your future self deserves financial comfort, freedom, and security, everything begins to align with that belief.

This belief is not about luck or magic; it is about mindset. It forms the foundation that guides your choices, motivates your habits, and keeps you steady through the ups and downs of money.

Why this habit matters:

- It fuels motivation. When you believe you deserve wealth, saving and budgeting become acts of self-care, not chores.
- It helps you bounce back from setbacks. Financial journeys are not always smooth, but belief in your worth keeps you moving forward.
- It opens your eyes to opportunity. You start to notice ways to grow your money and build value that you may have once overlooked.

- It strengthens confidence. Making financial decisions becomes easier when you know you're investing in your future happiness and security.

Try these money mindset boosters:

- Write down affirmations that remind you of your worth and wealth-building power.
- Surround yourself with people and stories that inspire financial confidence.
- Celebrate every small step as a proof that you are capable of building lasting wealth.

Remember, your future self is counting on you to make wise choices today. You are worthy of the time and effort required to build a solid financial foundation.

Believing that you deserve wealth is not wishful thinking; it is an active commitment to create the life you dream of.

Final Thoughts

Building healthy money habits is not about being perfect, it is about making small, steady steps toward a more secure, confident future.

Money can sometimes feel overwhelming or even intimidating, but it doesn't have to be that way. When you start treating money as a tool to support your goals and well-being, managing it becomes less stressful and more empowering. The key lies in consistency and being kind to yourself along the way.

Remember, it is not about how much you save or earn right now, but believing the fact that your future self deserves financial freedom and taking intentional steps to get there. Every small decision you make today sends a message of care and respect to your future. It is not about being rich. It is about feeling free.

Celebrate your small wins and show yourself grace when things don't go perfectly. Real growth comes from persistence, patience, and learning as you go. Your journey toward smarter money habits is an expression of self-love and self-respect.

Keep these habits close to yourself, revisit them often, and know that every step forward, no matter how small, brings you closer to the financial future you deserve.

Last Call to Action

You do not need a new year, a perfect plan, or anyone's permission to begin. Change often begins quietly—with a single decision, a subtle shift in awareness, and one moment of courage.

Over these pages, you have explored seventy-eight ways to bring more focus, clarity, and confidence into your life. However, this book is not a checklist—it is an invitation. Move through it at your own pace, pause where something resonates, and return whenever you need a reminder.

Growth is not about doing more; it is about doing what matters with greater intention. Let each habit reflect the person you are becoming—steadily, authentically, and on your own terms.

As you step forward, remember this:

- You define what success and fulfillment mean to you.
- You choose which habits stay and which ones fade.
- You are allowed to evolve beyond every version of who you've been.

No one else sets the pace of your journey. The world will always tell you to hurry, but real progress happens in quiet, steady persistence.

So take a breath. Trust your timing. Celebrate the steps no one sees.

Now, put these habits into practice and let them grow with you.

This is not the end. It is your next beginning.

[illegible] minutes [illegible]

let the [illegible] with [illegible]

[illegible]

About the Author

J.P. Adhikari, the pen name of *Jyoti Prasad Adhikari*, is an educator with a passion for personal transformation, introspection, and the quiet power of solitude. With a foundation in mathematics and a lifelong commitment to reflective living, he blends intellectual clarity with emotional depth to explore the human experience in its most authentic form. His work focuses on science education, mathematics, intentional living, and the act of returning to oneself in a world that rarely pauses.

In his quiet hours, Adhikari draws inspiration from nature and the inner rhythm of thought. He continues to explore how silence and self-inquiry can help shape a life of greater significance and authentic connection.

Other Self-help Book by the Author:

- *Echoroot: Reclaim the Gifts of Solitude*

Academic Book by the Author:

- *Partial Differential Equations: Foundations and Applications*

www.ingramcontent.com/pod-product-compliance
Ingram Content Group UK Ltd.
Pitfield, Milton Keynes, MK11 3LW, UK
UKHW011511190726
13845UKWH00034B/1203

9 788199 264526